ECHOES OF EAST ANGLIA

A SENTIMENTAL JOURNEY THROUGH PICTURES AND MEMORIES 1940–1945

MARTIN W. BOWMAN

HALSGROVE

First published in Great Britain in 2006

Title page: *During the war years Thorpe Abbots near Dickleburgh just off the A140 was home to the 'Bloody Hundredth' of the US
8th Air Force. Now the tower is a star attraction for visitors and the focal point for the 100th Bomb Group Memorial Museum, which
contains a wealth of momentoes and artifacts. Behind is the Horace L. Varian Visitor Centre, with its beautiful panoramic mural, a
refreshment bar and museum shop. During restoration of the tower in the 1970s and 1980s more than one volunteer experienced the eerie
noises of aircraft engines starting, radios crackling instructions and men shouting as a breeze suddenly came through the building!*

British Library Cataloguing-in-Publication Data
A CIP record for this title is available from the British Library

ISBN 1 84114 534 3
ISBN 978 1 84114 534 1

HALSGROVE
Halsgrove House
Lower Moor Way
Tiverton, Devon EX16 6SS
T: 01884 243242
F: 01884 243325
email: sales@halsgrove.com
website: www.halsgrove.com

Printed and bound by D'Auria Industrie Grafiche Spa, Italy

CONTENTS

PROLOGUE

…he walked through the winding old streets of Archbury direct to a pub called the Black Swan, borrowed a bicycle from the bartender, slung his package to the handlebars and pedaled out of the village along a country road lined with hedges and shaggy houses with thatched roofs. Presently he turned off on a side road, propped his bike against a hedge and strode slowly a hundred yards out onto an enormous flat, unobstructed field. When he halted he was standing at the head of a wide, dilapidated avenue of concrete, which stretched in front of him with gentle undulations for a mile and a half. A herd of cows, nibbling at the tall grass, which had grown up through the cracks, helped to camouflage his recollection of the huge runway. He noted the black streaks left by tires, where they had struck the surface, smoking. Nearby, through the weeds which nearly covered it, he could still see the stains left by puddles of grease and black oil on one of the hard-stands evenly spaced around the five-mile circumference of the perimeter track, like teeth on a ring gear. And in the background he could make out a forlorn dark green control tower, surmounted by a tattered gray windsock and behind it two empty hangars, a shoe box of a water tank on high stilts and an ugly cluster of squat Nissen huts. Not a soul was visible, nothing moved save the cows, nor was there any sound to break the great quiet. A gust of wind blew back the tall weeds behind the hardstand nearest him. But suddenly Stovall could no longer see the bent-back weeds through the quick tears that blurred his eyes and slid down the deep lines in his face. He made no move to brush them away. For behind the blur he could see, from within, more clearly. On each empty hard-stand there sat the ghost of a B-17, its four whirling propellers blasting the tall grass with the gale of its slip stream, its tires bulging under the weight of tons of bombs and tons of the gasoline needed for a deep penetration…'

Twelve O'Clock High

INTRODUCTION

By the end of the Second World War 360,000 acres of land had been occupied by airfields and a staggering 160 million square yards of concrete and tarmac had been laid down. Over 1000 airfields were used by the RAF in the UK alone, so it is with some justification that Britain was referred to as 'a vast aircraft carrier anchored off the north-west coast of Europe'. East Anglia had a great preponderance of these airfields, many of which had been built during the 1930s' expansion period for use by RAF Bomber, Fighter and Coastal Command squadrons in time of war. With America's entry into the conflict in late 1941 some stations were soon taken over by the USAAF but many more were needed for the Eighth Air Force. Air Ministry and American Engineer battalions cut a swathe through the furrowed fields of Norfolk, Suffolk and Cambridgeshire, leaving in their wake airfields destined for use by bomb wings and fighter groups. At first the USAAF had only 75 airfields in the United Kingdom but the total eventually reached 250 costing £645 million, £40 million of which was found by the American Government.

Home comforts were important to airmen whose lives were measured in weeks rather than months. Those lucky enough to be billeted at pre-war-built stations lived the high life when compared to those on the wartime bases where living conditions were often described as 'rugged'. Passing vehicles showered the men with mud as they walked and cycled from their Nissens to the mess halls and briefing rooms before take off. In winter interminable rain and fog so thick you had to cut it before you could walk made life unbearable and coal-fired stoves in the huts were totally inadequate at producing sufficient warmth for the 15-18 occupants. Coal was strictly rationed to one to two shovels full daily so the men usually saved this until night fell. Against strict orders they often made illegal sorties into local woods and cut off branches that would burn well. Chiefs of Staff, worried about the effect it could have on Anglo-American relations, issued a directive to end the practice.

High Command also took exception to the nudes that adorned the slim fighter fuselages and bombers' billboard-style bodies that served as the perfect canvas for artists and cartoonists. Double entendres like 'Miss Manooki' 'Virgin on the Verge", 'Miss Bea Havin' and 'Grin 'n Bare It' and epithets such as 'Red Ass' and 'Witches Tit' were considered too risqué but an official 'clean up' campaign proved in vain. Men simply responded to the 'dressing down' with negligees and skimpy bikinis more provocative than before!

Alas these fine aircraft and their paintings have long since been consigned to the melting pot but a few examples of

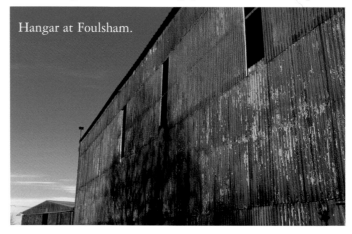

Hangar at Foulsham.

exuberant aircrews' imaginations survive on the walls of the barrack blocks, Quonsets and Nissens of the windswept and stark American bases and RAF stations that stand derelict and overgrown. Many murals were inspired by Gillette A. 'Gil' Elvgren's Brown & Bigelow Calendar Co. pin-ups, *Yank* magazine's full page photo pin-ups and George Petty's sinuous shapely ladies and Peruvian émigré Alberto Varga's aerodynamically sleek girls who appeared in *Esquire* magazine, which led the field with his scantily clad females. Needless to say, the 'Varga Girl' with her endless legs and perfect curves became the symbol of the serviceman's dreams.

When an inquisitive teenager armed with a Kodak Instamatic first chanced upon the lurid murals, pin-ups and cartoon characters in the early seventies they looked fresh and colourful. Swords had long been turned into ploughshares, many airfields had become industrial estates and the runways used for many purposes from racetracks to footings for turkey sheds while some huts housed pigs or stored hay for winter. By the 'noughties' time and the vagaries of the weather had eroded the majority of wall art. Most had faded from grace, some had lost their lustre completely but their aura lives on.

Echoes of East Anglia is a pictorial tribute to the thousands of young RAF and Commonwealth aircrews and their American cousins. For so many of them their East Anglian base was their last sight of England. As one explores these ghost airfields today, remember those men, women and machines that once thrived there.

Martin W. Bowman
Norwich, Norfolk

ONE – Wall to Wall

Bucking Bronco
formerly at Shipdham.

'The room in the Nissen hut was small, chill. A squat English stove struggled vainly to warm it. Less effective than a fire for display, it was only slightly more useful for heating. A small coalscuttle stood beside the stove. It was partly filled with coal and over the black lumps lay a sprinkling of cigarette butts and burned matches.

A map adorned one wall, a map of the United States with the signatures of flyers scrawled over their home states. Beneath the map was a rickety chair and against the other wall an iron cot. At the foot of the cot stood a foot locker with a water bucket on top of it, for shaving. A flight bag and a musette lay beside the footlocker. On a box built to serve as a desk was a coal-oil lamp for emergency use when the electricity failed during bombing raids.

At six the next morning, orderlies in hobnailed boots were stomping in double time up and down the upper hall banging on doors and bawling loudly. There was the tread of hurrying feet.

By six-thirty the mess was full. At the long tables were the flying officers, pilots, navigators and bombardiers, flanked by armament officers, meteorologists, radio officers and Intelligence men. Red-eyed and weary, the Intelligence officers were easy to spot. They had been up all night preparing the data for this mission.

Outside it was still dark. The ground mist was thick on the field. But above was a promise of clear skies and the "met" men confirmed it.

"This is it. Today we go."'

Major John M. Redding

A desolate scene with the pot-bellied stove in the middle of the Nissen. *'It was cold – the wet North Sea cold that was as nothing we had experienced before. It cut through six blankets at night and lay about the small coke stoves like wolves about a dying doe. We struggled and sweated over those stoves to warm, in part, our huts. It took an hour with wood to get the coke started and aglow, and the wood had to be stolen somewhere first.'*

The 'Yanks', as they were universally known, created a culture shock in the insular parishes of East Anglia. They came from the big cities and the backwoods, up state and down town, from California to Connecticut, the Deep South to Dixie, Delaware to Dakota, Frisco to Florida, Mid-West to Maine, the mighty Mississip' to Missouri, New York, New England, Ohio and Hawaii, the Pacific, Philly and the Rockies to the Rio Grande, from Texas to Tallahassee, Wyoming, Wisconsin, the Windy City and way beyond. **Martin Bowman**

'When not flying we usually ate four meals a day – breakfast, lunch and two dinners. We'd line up in the mess hall at about 0450 ready for the place to open at 0500. We'd then take a ride on our bicycles or otherwise kill time until just before they closed the doors at 0700. Each night as we headed for the mess hall at 0450 we heard the famous battle cry – "They're gonna feed 'em now!"'

Ronald D. Spencer

8th Air Force insignia at Bottisham, Cambridgeshire.

'Come and Get It!' 'We would don our flying coveralls' recalls Ben Smith, a B-17 radio operator, 'heated suits and boots and head to the mess hall down the road where the cooks were putting on a mission breakfast. The chefs were very solicitous, seemingly jovial. We could have pancakes, eggs sunny-side up or any way we wanted them. Sort of like, "It's your last meal. You can have what you want." To me it seemed a somewhat macabre occasion and I found their jollity very disquieting and out of place. I could eat none of the breakfast anyway. Even to this day I have butterflies before breakfast'.

'A messenger rode through the night on his GI English bicycle, stopping at our barracks housing four crews of enlisted men. He shone his flashlight (torch) on a cot where the engineer, Marcus DeCamp was barely awake. He answered when the messenger asked, "Walsh's crew?" The others in the adjoining beds heard but never really wanted to. We listened as he read his grisly message "Breakfast at 0430; Briefing at 0500; Start Engines at 0530; Taxi out at 0600 and take-off at 0630."

Each mission began with this harbinger of doom. One by one aircrews were awakened. To preserve oil in their skins as a protection against frostbite men did not wash or shave. The walk to the mess halls took about ten minutes depending on the weather. Inside there was a hubbub of conversation while the base kitchens served breakfasts of dehydrated eggs which came in square boxes, bread with apple butter, orange marmalade and black coffee. Sometimes we ate oatmeal and powdered milk; not because we liked it but because it was warm and filling. Food was prepared to eliminate indigestion and sickness at high altitude and anyway, it could be one's last meal for quite some time and we might have to walk home'.

Russ D. Hayes, ball-turret gunner

'At 5:50 in the morning we were awakened for our second mission. For breakfast it was lousy grapefruit juice, powdered eggs, hard crisp bacon, dried up toast and all this mixed with plenty of powdered milk. On top of this hot cakes with syrup that tasted like molasses. Then coffee for the short-winded crewmembers. We could even go back for seconds if you could get by the firsts.'

Joe Wroblewski, B-17 pilot

'...There were no fresh eggs at breakfast time; the only eggs available were powdered. These were prepared by being whipped into a great sticky emulsion, then apparently fried in axle grease left over from the needs of the motor pool; the result was a well-vulcanised, plastic lump of lukewarm goo. Milk also was available only in powdered form. We were warned in lectures by the Flight Surgeon's staff never to drink local milk in England but only to consume the GI powdered product. I found it unthinkable that a modern, civilised nation like Great Britain did not regulate the pasteurisation of milk but such seemed to be the case. I never did have the nerve to find out if the medicos were wrong.'

Jackson Granholm

At Horham airfield between Eye and Stradbroke in rural East Suffolk, the Red Feather Club, originally the 95th Bomb Group's NCO Mess, was saved from dereliction by a small group of enthusiasts who formed the Horham Airfield Heritage Association. Note that the electrical wiring doubles as strings on the cello!

'…The barracks required strenuous cleaning, the sanitary facilities were poor and those for bathing almost non-existent. The sites on which the various squadrons lived did not have bathhouses and the communal site with its one bathhouse was sadly overtaxed. Food upon the Group's arrival and for about four weeks was strictly British and the menus monotonously featured mutton, potatoes and Brussels Sprouts. On the other hand it was England – the England of the schoolbooks, of King Arthur and Robin Hood and Cromwell and for practically every member of the Group the first foreign country ever visited. It was also the beginning of the great adventure. Morale was buoyed up by an excitement that neither mud nor minor discomforts could dispel.'

John S. Sloan

The striking scenes at one end of the Red Feather Club at Horham with the knight on his white charger and the shield denoting the 95th Bomb Group.

A maidservant waiting at table in the Red Feather Club at Horham. American serviceman Nathan Bindler painted these superb murals.

14

Robin Hood and Little John in what was the American base library at Deopham Green airfield and which is now a carpentry shop.

'Life around the base now was beginning to be a bit move livable and, to some degree, like home. The Aero Club Lounge had been decorated by Cpl Ferris C. Parsons, Deep Sea murals to add a restful atmosphere. Mrs Holman Hunt added the interest in the library and Cpl Gerald E. Brown has painted Robin Hood scenes on the wall...The game room provided two pool tables, three ping pong tables and three dart boards. The room was decorated by Cpl Parsons' version of Donald Duck and Mickey Mouse, which was quite cute...All these things served to make life a bit more interesting and add to the joy of being in Merry Old England.'
452ⁿᵈ *BG History*

15

This fairy once fluttered above the serving hatch in the mess at Methwold.

Sadly this cartoon of a desert island character behind a palm tree in the Officers' Mess at Methwold disappeared when the roofless building was demolished soon after this photo was taken in about 1970. The station closed in 1963.

'…In Northampton the men went steadily to the Plough and the Angel, the Grand, the Swan, the Black Boy, the Queen's Arms and came out less steadily. The nightly liberty runs were loaded each way. The cyclists and the thumbers continued to go to Wellingborough. Billy Burke's Exchange Hotel drew a steady patronage; drawn perhaps equally by Mr Burke's undeniable charm and his woefully weak spirits.'

John S. Sloan

'On July 5 the long-awaited soda fountain was opened in the PX and although Coca-Cola was its only drink, queues of thirsty GIs were immediately in evidence. Decoratively, the fountain featured a South Seas motif complete with thatched roof and bamboo. Receipts from the fountain alone were £264 in 18 days – roughly over 21,000 glasses of real Coca-Cola sold.'

John S. Sloan

Foulsham airfield 15 miles north-west of Norwich in the parishes of Wood Norton and Foulsham and a half mile north of the village of the same name. The station closed in October 1945 and post war it was used by light aircraft and crop sprayers until in the mid-1980s the runways and other concrete areas were broken up. Currently the hangars remain on site but the control tower has been demolished. One of the T2 hangars has been used to hold bulk grain for an agricultural merchant: another is used by the Department of the Environment to store equipment and yet another by a warehousing company.

'A major improvement was made in the Consolidated Mess where a warmer color scheme, composed of grass green, primrose yellow and tangerine supplanted the old drab walls. Even warmer were the silhouette illustrations of female anatomy calculated to increase GI temperatures a few degrees. Wall decorations also included the names of famous combat aircraft and amusing color cartoons.'

John S. Sloan

Bottisham

18th Bomb Squadron, 34th Bomb Group insignia (now removed to Horham) at Mendlesham.

Here's a toast to those who love the vastness of the s

The Statue of Liberty, which once graced Bottisham, a Second World War American fighter base about 5 miles east of Cambridge. The dual carriageway to Newmarket and beyond now meanders across the centre of the airfield.

'In the lobby of the Administration Building of the Field, some talented RAF pilot stationed there had painted a striking series of murals, pictures in vivid colors of all the places to which airplanes fly today. Landscapes in vivid jungle green, with crocodiles in the foreground and a Skymaster splitting the horizon; the skyline of New York City from LaGuardia Airport; kangaroos in another foreground; a native wearing nothing but a basket of bananas on her head; camels in another panel of the mural, with beautiful Arab women in the foreground. Heavy emphasis on the women in all the panels…'

Captain John R. 'Tex' McCrary

Mural of Stirling III of 199 Squadron at North Creake, which in 1983 was carefully removed and put on permanent display in the RAF Bomber Command Museum at Hendon. Underneath the mural is the inscription 'Chop 16-6-44 R.I.P.' which refers to the night of 16/17 June 1944 when this aircraft disappeared in the North Sea with Sergeant Watts and crew.

RAF wings at Fowlmere, a wartime satellite airfield for Duxford. (Bill Espie)

TWO – GHOST STORIES

'If as war does occur it may be very well be that the larger houses of this country will play a more important part then they have ever played before in our national history.'

Earl Beauchamp

'Jane', the famous *Daily Mirror* strip cartoon character still survives in the haunted former cinema at Swanton Morley.

In 1432, Sir John Fastolfe, a famous soldier, who Shakespeare altered slightly for his comic hero Falstaff, purchased Blickling Hall. Fastolfe died at Caister Castle in 1459, having sold Blickling to Geoffrey Boleyn. Tradition has it that his daughter, Anne Boleyn (1507-36), second wife of Henry VIII and mother of Elizabeth I of England, was born at Blickling. Beheaded in the Tower of London, her ghost is said to haunt the Hall. Lord Lothian, who had been the British ambassador to the USA until his death in 1940, had left the house and grounds to the National Trust. When the RAF took over part of Blickling Hall they occupied the barns to the east of the west wing and used accommodation in the private rooms at the rear of the hall. High in the attics, where sixteenth century maids had slept in small rooms, now slept the 'erks', batmen, and flight sergeants. The Harness Room became a guardroom. Lord Lothian's fearsome secretary, Miss O'Sullivan, nicknamed 'Mrs. Danvers' (in *Rebecca*) or, just simply, 'the Dragon' ensured that the RAF remained in their allotted area! It is reputed that the RAF officers were more frightened of her than they were of their CO!

'…we had landed in a veritable Garden of Eden. The officers' living quarters were located in a beautifully wooded area of Blickling Park, a stone's throw from Blickling Hall, a magnificent seventeenth-century Jacobean mansion. This large and beautiful estate belonged to the Marquis of Lothian but a substantial portion of it had been taken over for the duration by the RAF…The grounds were steeped in history. Long before the great Hall had been built the property had belonged to Anne Boleyn's father and the local legend was that the ill-fated young Queen had spent many happy hours on this spot. It went on to suggest that on particularly dark nights one might anticipate a ghostly encounter with her, walking around the lovely little lake bordering the mansion accompanied by her great mastiff - but walking in the somewhat handicapped manner suggested in the old song, i.e. *"with 'er 'ead tooked oonderneath 'er arm."'*

Canadian Flight Lieutenant Murray Peden DFC QC, pilot, 214 Squadron

The haunted cinema with the projection holes blocked off.

NO SMOKING

Artwork still surviving in the haunted cinema. The wartime artist cleverly painted lighthouses so that the light beams shone from the apertures for the projectionist's movie cameras.

Girl and duck cartoons in the haunted cinema

The haunted cinema.

A fireplace in the former RAF guard house at Blickling Hall still showing details of library opening times.

'We were at Blickling from Sept. 42 to the summer of 43; a most wonderful period on several levels; high drama in terms of the war and the seductive delights of a country mansion during the quiet moments.'

Jack Peppiatt, RAF pilot

Three Stearman biplanes passing picturesque Blickling Hall where RAF personnel were fortunate to be billeted during operations from Oulton nearby. The Sergeants' Mess was in what is now the Steward's Room, the entrance being in the SW corner of the Hall, while the Officers' Mess was in the East Wing of the Hall with the entrance in the SE corner. Evidence of the RAF occupation, which included access to the lake for swimming and dinghy drills, can still be found today.

'...The Sergeants' Mess was situated in what is now the Steward's Room, the entrance being in the southwest corner of the Hall. The Officers' Mess was located in the East Wing of the Hall with the entrance in the southeast corner. The main entrance and the staircase were not accessible to us but the remainder of the Hall and all of the grounds were our "home". The beauty of the Hall was not lost on me but being a native of Wensleydale it was the lake and grounds, which were for me the greatest asset. At that time we were under a great deal of stress and the peace and tranquillity in which we found ourselves was an ideal setting in which to unwind. In the basement by the kitchen on the west side of the Hall was the telephone exchange. I can still picture cheese sandwiches waiting in the Mess for our attention on returning from an evening out. It was quite a pleasant summer and we regularly swam in the lake under the disapproving eye of the resident swan. We had no licensed bar so the Buckinghamshire Arms became out "local" if we didn't have the desire to sample the "fleshpots" of Norwich or Aylsham.

My nineteen-year-old brother Peter, who had just qualified as an electrician, was posted to the Squadron. His quarters were in a dormitory, above what is now the restaurant. He also worked on the Flight with which I flew and it must have been very traumatic for him when we were flying on operations. Despite this experience in August 1942 he re-mustered as an air gunner, losing his life on his first operation on 28 May 1943.'

**Twenty-year-old Jim Moore DFC,
wireless operator/air gunner who lived at
Blickling Hall in April 1941 and again
in September 1942 until 31 March 1943**

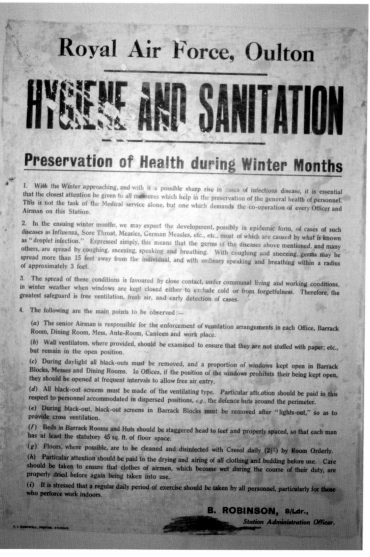

Hygene and sanitation notice for RAF personnel at Oulton in part of the former servants' quarters in the upper floor of Blickling Hall.

The Old Rectory adjacent to Bexwell Church once served as the Officers' Mess for aircrews from Downham Market. Inside the church is a memorial tablet to squadrons that operated from the airfield and the memorial in the churchyard includes detailed inscriptions leading to the award of posthumous VCs to Arthur Aaron DFM and Ian Bazalgette DFC RAFVR. Airmen at Downham Market found The Carpenters Arms in Denver 'a most welcoming and hospitable' pub and the 'Chippies' soon became one of the aircrews' favourite 'targets for tonight' when they were not flying. It is now a private residence.

'It happened on an airfield sometime in the war
A bomb upon the peri-track exploded with a roar
Of course there was a crater and also men were killed;
But the airfield it was needed and so the hole was filled.
War ended and that airfield became a track to race
Motor-bikes and motor-cars at tremendous pace,
It has a bend called "Bomb-hole", the spot of that explosion
Which some believe inherits spooky soil erosion
For no matter how it's treated to make it level, flat
Soon it is appearing anything but that
Then of course the temperature! That needs some explaining?
For no matter in a heatwave, thunderstorm, or raining,
If you are in "T" shirt as you sit in pit or stand,
But going down to Bomb-hole, take a jacket in your hand
For there's ghostly presence, though I doubt it bids you ill,
It fixes that location with a supernatural chill.'

Snetterton, by Jasper Miles

Runways to race tracks. 'War ended and that airfield became a track to race, Motor-bikes and motor-cars at tremendous pace.' Snetterton Heath is one of several airfields in Britain, which has been put to recreational use. It boasts a fine memorial to the American 96th Bomb Group based here in the Second World War and a Sunday market is held every week.

The type of hangar on RAF and American wartime airfields varied but the T2, a rectangular, steel-framed 240-foot-long building, 39 feet high and 120 feet span, clad with corrugated steel sheet and with sliding doors at each end, was the most numerous.

'One summer evening when everyone else had left the airfield I spent an hour in the hangar at Tibenham trying to free a wheel on a lifting-trolley. Eventually I had to admit defeat. Then I heard a quiet American voice beside me offering assistance and advice and almost immediately afterwards we levered the tyre free. He stayed a while and talked of B-24s and Jimmy Stewart but I neither saw him arrive nor depart and certainly neither heard nor saw a car. I took crumpled wheel fairing to the work-shop and set to work with the hammer. Minutes later I heard someone whistling a tune and obviously approaching along the corridor. Hammer poised, I waited to greet the visitor but the whistling passed the open door – though no one appeared. Puzzled, I looked out along the empty corridor and then into each of the rooms before doing a circuit outside the building. There was nobody so I tried to convince myself that I had imagined it all and went back to the bench. Three times I heard that whistling and three times I searched the building to no avail. Weeks later I was told how one night a Ju 88 followed the Liberators back to their base, shot down three in the circuit and caused two more to collide. I also heard that there was supposed to be a ridiculous tale about the ghost of one of the navigators who was known to haunt the control tower.'

Charles Hall

The old control tower at Debach has now been restored and is a museum.

'A lonely figure walked to where a runway ended,
Thoughts deep in the past as his spirit blended.
Seeing this airfield as he once knew it.
Remembering well! He'd flown, and lived
   through it.
Exorcising ghosts, he roamed o'er the acres,
Recalling faces, nicknames, of givers and takers.
Pilots, navs and flight engineers too
Wireless ops, gunners, from each motley crew.'
Old Bomber Base Revisited;
A Pilot's Pilgrimage to the Past,
Jim McCorkle RAF, pilot

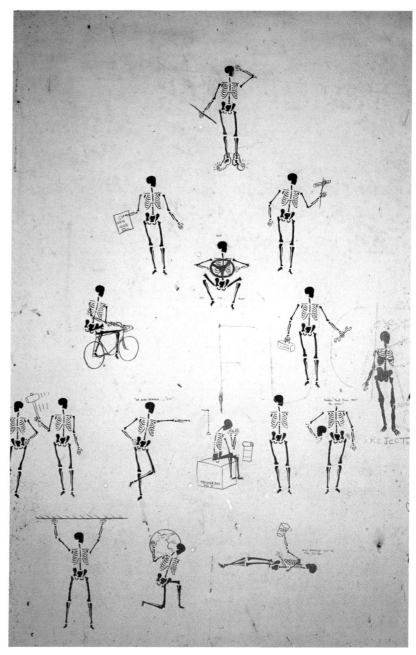

Skeletons at RAF Twinwood's control tower, which is now a museum. It is claimed that on 15 December 1944 a Norseman stopped off here to pick up famous band leader Major Glenn Miller to fly him to Paris although no record of the departure in the control tower log nor any evidence of the flight has ever been produced.

Shipdham airfield 3 miles south of East Dereham was the first US heavy bomber base in Norfolk and was also continuous host to B-24 Liberators longer than any other Eighth Air Force airfield in Britain, from October 1942 to June 1945. It was built in 1941-42 at a total cost of £1,100,000 to the standard Air Ministry design for bomber fields with three intersecting runways, encircling taxiway and aircraft dispersal points, all concrete with macadam surfacing.

At Shipdham several industries occupy the three T2 hangars on the south side where the technical site once was. The control tower has partially restored and though far from complete, it is still standing.

'England was always out the
– Bert Stiles, *Serenade to The Big Bird*.
Bassingbourn viewed from the control
tower. This airfield, built originally as a
grass aerodrome for the RAF in a very
shallow, wide valley north of Royston
opened in 1938 though the American
91st Bomb Group was in residence
throughout the war years. Now a British
Army Infantry Training Depot, the pub
is named the *Memphis Belle* after one of
the most famous Flying Fortresses of the
war, which flew missions from
Bassingbourn until May 1943 when it
returned home to the USA and a hero's
welcome.

'A Norfolk native who frequents the old
airfields in the region told me that on
moonlit nights one can drive around the
abandoned perimeter tracks of the
airfields and feel the presence of those
who have gone before, the airplanes and
the men. He said it always happens that
as one of the bombers that was lost, a
mysterious quiet descends on the scene
and there's no sound not even that of the
night birds singing. Ghosts haunt those
areas and the runway. I know because I
have felt them and they do not let one
pass without making themselves
known.'

Forrest S. Clark, B-24 gunner

The now demolished RAF mess in woods at the former Methwold airfield north of Brandon, Suffolk. The first recorded flying ground in the parish of Methwold was during the First World War when a Royal Flying Corps military night landing ground was sited here in early 1916 and was possibly within the boundary of the Second World War airfield.

Ketteringham Hall 7½ miles to the SW of Norwich near to Hethel airfield, which, from December 1943 to June 1945 was used as an American AAF Headquarters. The Hall dates from Tudor times and is reputed to have been the childhood home of Lady Jane Grey (1537 1554), England's shortest-reigning monarch. After the war the hall served as a prep school and it was bought by Lotus Cars in 1968.

'Most
miss seeing Eddie's ghost
He sits there oh so still
and probably never will
notice those who pass
his spot in the grass.
Time, for Eddie, ceased in 'forty-four,
he had just two missions more
before returning home Stateside
to take Pauline as his bride;
always showing folks her photograph:
it made his buddies laugh.
After mail-call that day
he was seen to walk away
like he did not want to know
and alone sat down where daisies grow.
Then came the forty-five's loud bang
and men raced to where it rang.
"Shit! Eddie's shot himself! Hell why?"
a friend was heard to cry.
But then he understood better,
picking up and reading Pauline's "Dear John" letter.'

Eddie's Ghost by Jasper Miles

Elveden Hall with its huge copper dome bursting out of a green mass of trees, in Elveden village 4 miles southwest of Thetford, was bought by Lord Iveagh from an Indian maharaja in 1894 and was a wartime American HQ. The stables were converted into airmen's quarters. Inside, the carved staircase was protected by plywood; the Countess's boudoir was converted into a War Room with an Operation Room next door. A church on the edge of the estate beside the A11 contains a superb stained glass window in honour and memory of the members of the Third Air Division and shows an American airman kneeling humbly beneath the wings of an angel with hangars and USAAF aircraft under the shade of English oaks.

Bylaugh Hall viewed through the missing panes of a Nissen hut window.

'Part of the time the whole squadron was billeted in Bylaugh Hall. Going down to the airfield in RAF coaches each day or riding service bikes and it was absolute luxury at the Hall. At the entrance were two columns surmounted by stone balls, one of which lay on the ground. One night, when we were all in bed, around midnight, there was a right roar as if a hell of a thunderstorm had started. Some aircrew had come in, rolled the loose ball up the stone entrance steps, then down the spiral stone steps leading to the servants' quarters in the cellar to eventually crash through somebody's bedroom door!'

Harry Castledine, fitter IIA

Bylaugh Hall near Swanton Morley airfield was a wartime RAF HQ for 2 Group and 100 Group.

'At Swanton our reception was cold, our sleeping quarters at Bylaugh Hall were cold and primitive, our first meal diabolical - cold brown Windsor soup followed by boiled chicken so tough it squeaked when cut with a knife. After dinner the anteroom fire was blocked by a bridge quartet of the permanent staff who angrily shushed our singing and drinking party. 'Digger' Wheeler, my No.2, an incredibly tough New Zealander who had been sheep ranching in the Argentine, in a friendly wrestling match, threw me across the hall floor, then polished oak and I fetched up on the leg of a piano on the far side. I rose to my feet with a jet of arterial blood pumping from a cut in my fore-head. "Squadron leader" said he, "I think you had better cut off to sick quarters."'

Squadron Leader
John Castle, pilot

The Hall, which spent many years in a derelict conditon with the roof missing, has now been fully restored to its former glory. Nearby in stark contrast to the renovation are a few rusting skeletal Nissen huts, many overgrown and minus their window panes.

Ye Olde ERKS CASINO at Langham in the early 1970s.

44

The former fire station beside the control tower at Lavenham.

'Through what had been an airbase I chanced to drive one night
when a white ceramic toilet came to view
The sky was almost cloudless and the moon was shining bright
which made this aged receptacle seem new
Either new or ghostly but there was no fear
no chill and no other indication spooks were near
And I know spectral bodies have not the need nor
will for visiting of toilets to park the astral rear
But the toilet in its glory, alone, bereft of wall,
raised one foot above the ground, was standing like complete
Alas without a cistern, no pipe, no chain at all,
and some damned thief had stole its wooden seat…'
Solitary Toilet, Jasper Miles

Last Post. An outhouse at Wendling

THREE – The Hut

The Holly and the Ivy at Shipdham.

Nissen in the snow. The Nissen hut was invented in 1915 by a Canadian, Colonel P. N. Nissen, who died in March 1930.

'We were a mixed bag. Probably for the first time in our young lives, we found ourselves working alongside people from all over the place. They were fine young men. Our numbers included chaps from New Zealand, Australia, West Indies, Canada, Argentina; from Scotland, Ireland and Wales…The buildings in which we lived and worked were all very temporary, many of them Nissen huts with tin roofs. Hot in summer and freezing cold in winter, despite their stoves for which there was never enough coal; and not very comfortable at the best of times. And yet, I really cannot remember anybody moaning about them.'

Squadron Leader (later Grp Capt) A. F. Wallace

Rackheath control tower.

'The Air Ministry had built our base. Its plan was far different from that of American bases. There were no serried rows of bleak buildings with grass and trees scraped from the ground and everything barren, efficient and a scar on the landscape. Rackheath had benefited from the necessities of camouflage. Nissen huts were grouped under tall trees at the edge of woods and in and under them. Roads passed under rows of fruit trees. The farm croft and byre were left untouched. One site was far down by the rhododendron drive, another across the Jersey pasture where the ornamental sheep and tame deer grazed. You walked through a bluebell-carpeted wood in spring from Site 1 to the Operations Block and past straw ricks from there to the Briefing Building. A hedgerow lined the lane of a civilian-travelled road right through the base, where, on Sundays, the children stood and asked, "Any gum, chum?" Much of the farm-like quality of the countryside was preserved so that from the air only the slash of the runways showed.'

Allan Healy

'…There used to be a gnome-like Irishman who came around to the barracks with fresh eggs for sale. One night he appeared with a bottle of Jameson's Irish whiskey, which he sold us for $10. After he had gone we poured ourselves a drink in our mess cups and to our chagrin found out it was cold tea. Needless to say we never saw the little Irishman again.'

George M. Collar, US airman

'When we asked, "Why the empty beds?" we were told they were left by the men who had gone down recently. This was rather discouraging.'

Larry Goldstein, radio operator

Construction of an American bomber base for the 467th Bomb Group at Rackheath 5 miles northeast of Norwich began in late 1942 on a natural plateau near Sir Edward Stracey's estate (in the foreground). The plentiful woodland and general agricultural features were deliberately preserved and helped to camouflage the base. During construction of the airfield, 556,000 cubic yards of soil were excavated, 14,000 yards of soakaway drains installed and 504,000 yards of concrete laid. In the distance are the Norfolk Broads.

Solitary Nissen. In the Second World War Nissen huts were purchased in bulk from the manufacturers and supplied to aerodromes by the Air Ministry.

'When we arrived at our Quonset hut, so many officers had been killed there was no room to hang our clothes. One door was blocked with piles of uniforms. In the interim, our crew borrowed a wheelchair from supply and moved clothing and foot-lockers out. It took us two days to empty the barracks.'

John A. Holden, navigator

Nissen hut ravaged by Old Father Tyme.

'We landed and it was just pouring with rain. It had been light rain just shortly before and we got on the ground and got over to our dispersal area, and I mean it just opened up about three faucets; it just came down in buckets. I didn't know what to think of it. The buildings were so unusual; most of 'em were Quonset huts.'

Technical Sergeant Walt Hagemeier Jr., radio operator

'It seems like a dream but the empty bunks in our barracks prove it is not. Yesterday we attended the funerals of our fellow crewmen whom we learned to love as brothers.'

Sgt Arthur Dobias, waist gunner

The Briefing Hut at Knettishall (now demolished).

RAF hut at Swannington airfield about 8 miles northwest of Norwich, construction of which began in October 1942. Haveringland Hall, which was requisitioned for an officers' mess is now no more.

'Home for the bomber crew officer personnel in our squadron was a Nissen hut accom-
modating twelve crewmembers or four
crews, each consisting of a pilot, co-pilot,
and navigator. The hut was small, approxi-
mately 20 by 30 feet, with a concrete floor
and the typical corrugated steel hemispheri-
cal construction. A small vestibule with
double doors (for blackout protection) was
supposedly located at one end. A single door
provided access at the other end. Warmth in
cold weather (which it usually was) was
supposedly provided by a small stove
located in the center. Government Issue fuel
consisted of large chunks of coal, actually
coke. We quickly found that you could
consume the whole weekly allotment of 52
pounds of coke in one day if you wanted to
keep the hut comfortable.'

Ronald D. Spencer

'The huts were lined but not insulated so
were pretty cold in the wintertime. Rats
would get in between the lining and when
things got dull we'd chase them out to shoot
at with our .45s – never hit any. We had a
coke burner in the middle of the room and
when it was going the ones near it cooked
while the ones at the ends froze – when we
had fuel that is.'

Ralph Elliott

Many wartime buildings continue to withstand each seasonal onslaught of biting
winds, torrential rain, driving snow and freezing ice with only occasional winter
sunshine to warm their insides. Rusting window frames and broken panes testify
to the harsh environment that one day will finally overcome dogged resistance
and they will give up the ghost and sadly surrender to the inevitable.

'Who can forget these ghosts of the airfields?'

'Another facet of hut life was the diverse life styles of the various inhabitants. You had the swingers, the club hounds, the pub crawlers, the sack rats who never left their beds except to fly or to eat, the eager beavers who followed every rule and restriction to the letter, the neatniks, the slobs, etc, etc. Conflicts often arose because of the differing personalities…'

Ronald D. Spencer

December sun going down near Maycrete huts at Lavenham. The cost of a typical Ministry of Works 10-bay hut including carriage, foundations and erection, was £390.

The setting sun framed in a window at Lavenham.

'About one night a week we'd receive a RAF plane low on fuel or damaged, returning from a mission over Germany. We accused those "blokes" of stopping by just to one of our hearty breakfasts of dehydrated eggs made with dehydrated milk and flavored with dehydrated bacon bits/ what they enjoyed most was to layer on to our "home-baked" bread several of the myriad of jams, jellies, peanut butter, marmalade and apple butter found on each mess hall table. Occasionally, some of our GI blankets, warmer than the RAF issue, departed with them in the morning.'

Lt Colonel James J. Mahoney

The fire has long since gone out. Airmen trying to keep warm once gathered here on cold winter nights to burn coke and boughs from trees.

'It was cold – the wet North Sea cold that was as nothing we had experienced before. It cut through six blankets at night and lay about the small coke stoves like wolves about a dying doe. We struggled and sweated over those stoves to warm, in part, our huts. It took an hour with wood to get the coke started and aglow and the wood had to be stolen somewhere first.'

Allan Healy

'During the really cold weather, everyone requisitioned (stole) extra blankets in an effort to keep warm. At one time I had nine.'

Ronald D. Spencer

'I moved my gear into a barracks and threw it onto one of the lower bunks which was conveniently near one of the two warm 'pot-bellied' stoves. One of the men said, "You can take that bunk if you want but it belonged to our engineer, who got it through the head on a mission a couple of days ago."

With no further words I selected another bunk, farther away from the heat of the stove.'

William C. Stewart, air gunner

'The crew that we resided with were on their 28th or 29th mission and they were all crazy. One in particular would wake up in the middle of the night and shoot his .45 off at mice. A .45 reverberates and makes quite a bit of noise and disturbs your sleep!'

John A. Holden, navigator

Crew 51's mission log painted inside a SECO hut at Rackheath by Sergeant Jack Hallman, a combat crew gunner whose bed would have been close by.

'Like most Nissen huts those at RAF Foulsham were equipped with two large black cast-iron coke-burning stoves for heating. During winter these were barely adequate to warm this living/sleeping accommodation. To generate maximum heat it was necessary to burn plenty of wood, acquired by whatever means and to keep the chimney pipe out through the roof clear of soot. Both the former and latter were executed with aplomb by the members of one hut occupied by members of 462 Squadron RAAF. Collecting the timber was a doddle. On the face of it chimney cleaning presented the greater challenge. However, this was accomplished with equal dexterity by lighting a fire, dropping a Very cartridge into the stove, abandoning the hut and waiting for the massive 'whoosh' as the cartridge exploded driving the soot and contents of the fire out through the top of the chimney pipe! After which the fire roared-away without hindrance for a couple of months!'   **Group Captain J. A. V. Short**

Hangar at Foulsham.

Foulsham airfield in the 1990s. The Class A type airfield consisted of three intersecting runways, with the main runway aligned to the prevailing wind, being 2000 yards long and the other two 1400 yards long. Each runway was standardized at fifty yards wide and a 50ft wide perimeter track or taxiway encircled the runway and joined the end of each. Branching off the taxiways were fifty hardstands and dispersal points for the aircraft.

Hedenham Hall a wartime combat rest and recuperation centre on the Norwich to Bungay road has now been converted to flats. 'The Bronco Bar' in the former stable at the rear of the Hall had paintings of various aircraft on its walls.

'A somewhat vicious trick carried out by the Australians returning from an evening drinking session was to select a bed occupied by someone less than generally popular. The perpetrators would then pour Ronsonol lighter fuel across the blanket at the bottom of the bed. This would be ignited at the same time as the sleeping occupant was awakened with the cry, "Excuse me mate but your bed is on fire!"'

Group Captain J. A. V. Short

Traces of a B-24 crewman's mission log above what would have been his bed, in a former barrack hut at Seething.

'We had four officer crews in one Nissen hut. One night one of the officer crews packed all their belongings. It made me wonder what insight they must have had when they knew they would not survive the next mission. Sure enough, the next day they went down.'

Bill Rose, pilot

Construction of Foulsham airfield began in 1941 and was almost complete by the late summer of 1942. Eventually seven hangars – six T2s like this one, and a B1 were erected on the main technical area on the east side of the airfield. Another T2 was built on the southwest side near Wades Farm and two more T2s on the southeast corner by Millhill Farm.

A rusting tractor beside wood staves propping up a hut threatening to subside concertina fashion at Swannington.

This solitary building at Shipdham airfield was once the base morgue.

Air raid shelter, which now has a tree blocking entry!

'Our first combat breakfast was powdered eggs. There was very little conversation at breakfast or on the trip to the briefing room.'

Alvin Skaggs, pilot

Overgrown entrance to a Nissen hut at Great Ashfield in 1997

'At the mess hall a bedlam greeted us as we entered the door. The smoke of burning grease assailed our nostrils and smarted in our eyes as we filed in for our "real fresh eggs". Perhaps a slice or two of salty bacon also on the plate and to a table for the first problem: Can I get them down? After a drink of grapefruit or tomato juice it usually became easier but it didn't take much to satiate our appetites that morning! Each mouthful became an additional lump of lead in the pit of our stomachs and we were soon ready to board the truck that would take us to briefing.' **Lieutenant Robert 'Roco' Work, navigator**

FOUR –
Erogenous Zones

Nude that once adorned the briefing hut at Raydon in the Second World War and is now stored at Duxford.

'Life at Swanton Morley – a hellspot only 15 miles from Norwich but which might well have been in deepest Siberia – began sedately enough…Dullish days but nights were duller still, as for recreation, romance and merriment one had to rely on nearby East Dereham where mothers locked away their daughters after tea and every door slammed tight shut on the dot of 1800hrs. Nothing to do but go shivering to our beds in our freezing Nissen huts. Excitement was somewhat lacking…..'

Sergeant Mike Carreck DFC

'We had extra cigarette rations. Ultra-violet lamps were provided for our use. If we tried we could appear tanned and healthy even if we weren't. It was no wonder that aircrew were the favourites of the young girls, lonely wives and widows of surrounding districts. But it was rather like fattening turkeys for Christmas; they didn't call him "Butch" Harris for nothing.'

Ron Read

The former RAF Swanton Morley with the main camp top left of the grass airfield, now an Army Barracks. Centre right is a T2 hangar which was used during the war as a servicing facility for Mosquito aircraft.

American graffiti at Great Ashfield, which in the Second World War was a base for Flying Fortresses of the 385th Bomb Group.

'On one occasion I woke old George and "Gentleman" Jim at 5 a.m. for the practice mission...not realizing they had a couple of girls in the sack with them...and was met by a barrage of .45 gunshots over my head in the dark...I hit the floor of the hallway and crawled out! They were quite a bunch and when they were gone there was no-one who ever quite took their places.'

Lieutenant (later Colonel) William Cameron

'The Enlisted Men's Bar and Lounge suffered a slight decline in patronage due to the weather. Nevertheless, an ambitious Sunday Club Matinee policy was established with the Red Cross Aeroclub collaborating in the furnishing of girls from neighboring towns. The experiment was enthusiastically received.'

John S. Sloan

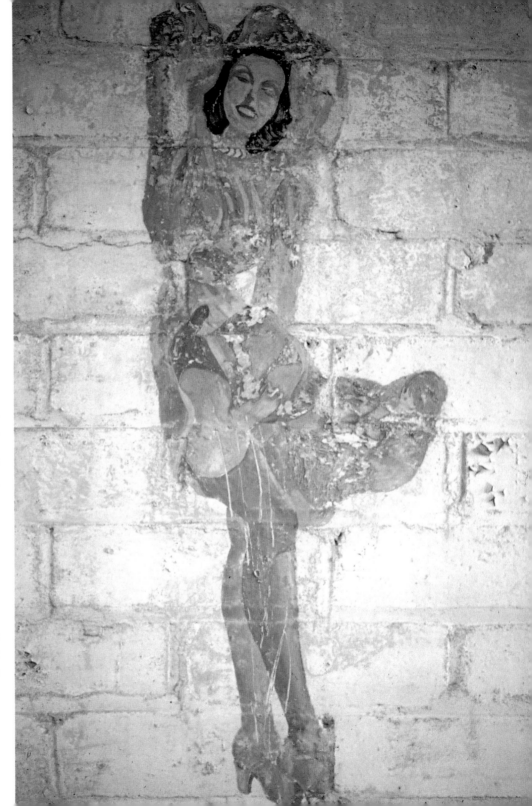

'Once a month, we had a party at the officers club. Eight or ten trucks were sent to the neighboring villages to pick up the young ladies that were eager to entertain or be entertained by those daring combatants. Americans seemed to fascinate these gals. Many of them would love to have married an American and come state side or as they would put it, move to the colonies.' **R. H. Tays**

American crews christened their aircraft with the names of their sweethearts and risked the wrath of their superiors painting risqué double entendres like 'Virgin on the Verge' and scantily clad 'Varga' and 'Petty' girls inspired by Esquire Magazine. Naturally, the pin-ups adorned the back of American A-2 flying jackets and the walls of their huts too.

Pin-up, one of several at the 14th Combat Wing HQ by Jack Loman using paint bought at Jarrold's department store in Norwich in 1943.

Pin-ups like this one at Wendling, Norfolk owed their origins to several sources. *Men Only, Look* and *Yank*, the GI's own news magazine, ran full-page photo pin-ups such as Betty Grable, Chilli Williams in her two-piece polka dot bathing suit, Lana Turner, Alexis Smith and Rita Hayworth in a silk negligee. Also there were George Petty's gatefolds, Gil Elvgren's stunning girls and Alberto Vargas's timeless beauties. Vargas 'who could make a girl look nude if she were rolled up in a rug' eclipsed them all as *Esquire* sent special military editions and calendars to all theatres of war.

Wine, women and song?
Wendling in the early 1980s.

'...I went to Bovingdon, near Watford, west of London for indoctrination to the European Theater of Operations, including how to get along with the English people. We should never, never say "bloody" in polite company. They did not prepare me, nevertheless for what I soon saw in the park at Watford during evening hours. Nor did they tell me how to ask an English girl politely if she wanted to make love. That remained for a new acquaintance of mine. After our first outing to a dance in Cambridge he advised that the proper words a girl had told him were: "I say, let's 'ave a go," and "'ow about an on?" My God, I thought, don't the English speak American? I think he fibbed in using that Cockney accent. Cambridge is not in Cockney land. Besides, the East Anglian girl I married within the year never talked like that, not bloody likely!'

Robert H. Shaver

A GI thinly disguised as a 'wolf' eyeing a pin-up who has snagged her stockings on the barbed wire at Shipdham. (The 'A' on the barrack bag denotes the 44th Bomb Goup identification letter.

> 'Yankee officers cause us to smile,
> With their light pants, you see them for miles,
> We wonder if they're mice or men,
> Decided they're wolves; we avoid the den.'
>> *The GIs*, by a WAAF at Shipdham

A 'dame' on a bar stool in the bar room mural at Shipdham.

'The young lady wants to see her boyfriend's bomber. She is curious about the name *Frenesi*. She asks the young sergeant what the name means. He replies, "Oh you know, it's from the title of the song, Frenesi. She hesitates and says, "Oh, you Yanks can't fool me. Frenesi means free and easy — and that's the way you like your girls."

Abel L. Dolim

'The visit of two British ladies to the airbase. They were mother and daughter and both were obviously pregnant. The other parent in each case was, they alleged, a sergeant named "Billy" — no last name specified. But they were not unhappy about Billy's expertise in bed — their complaint was that he had stolen their bicycles and they had not seen him since…'

Jackson Granholm

'Jane', pin-up heroine of the *Daily Mirror* strip cartoon, in an office in the haunted building, which was once a cinema. A young girl who left alone for a while, said later that the 'lady' had 'talked to her'. The owner's dog will not set foot in this office.

'As we left our sparsely furnished rooms to start our final preparations, we would take a last look around – perhaps at the bedside locker with its family photographs. Most of us were single; some would have a picture of the girlfriend or Betty Grable or "Jane" of the *Daily Mirror*. Some were married and the pictures would be of the wife and perhaps children and Betty Grable and "Jane". There might just have been that lingering thought: "I wonder if I'll see them again?"'

Squadron Leader
(later Grp Capt)
A. F. Wallace

A pin-up now displayed at the 100th Bomb Group Memorial Museum at Thorpe Abbots

'We gave parties in the Red Cross Club kitchen when a crew finished 30 missions – fried eggs… For the group's 200th mission they sent me out to recruit GIRLS. The first place I went a stern WREN officer said, "No". "Didn't the girls have a good time at the 100th mission party?" I asked. I guess they did. She said it was several days before she got them back!'

Mary Carroll Leeds, American Red Cross

'…Most people hung out in the club on the base as opposed to pubbing or going into Norwich. Also, the officers' club had so much money in the treasury that they began handing out free beer and sandwiches later in the evening. That was enough of an incentive to stay on the base. Another was the occasional party where girls were brought in from town in a bus or buses. The big problem was getting them off the base after the party. Our base was pretty straight in that regard. But some bases were notoriously lax. On one, I was told, they put up a sign on the following Monday saying that all women will positively be off the base by Thursday – I guess to get ready for the following Saturday night's influx.'

Ronald D. Spencer

Flamenco dancer and guitarist which now have all-but disappeared at Shipdham.

'Parties at the club usually produced a fair amount of food and drink, obviously one of the incentives for the young ladies to come to the parties. Also, it was warm in the club, a rarity in wartime England. A specialty at the parties was "Moose Juice", a concoction of medicinal alcohol and grapefruit juice. It tasted like straight grapefruit juice and thus was rather insidious. I remember drinking a couple of cups of the stuff and not much else till I awoke the next morning with a terrible hangover. I had no recollection of how I got home.'   **Ronald D. Spencer**

The stage is set but sadly, these 6ft high dancing girls at Deopham Green disappeared in the late seventies when the building was demolished.

'The Americans became part of us. You wouldn't want to mix with a nicer bunch of fellows. That's why I got married when I did. I knew that if I didn't nab my girl, they would.'

**Bill Eady, twenty-two, Elms Farm, Lavenham
who had 2900 Americans for neighbours**

'...Rumor has it a small group of renegades had stashed a blonde and a redhead in one of the Nissens for nearly a week....'
Abel L. Dolim

84

'The aircrews preparing for the day's mission are really ticked off. The word has been passed on to clean up the bare-assed ladies on the bombers. They will be required to have panties – at least. Already the bomber names have been cleaned up — B-17 "TWATS IT TO YOU?" has been renamed "?IT TO YOU?" And what is worse, rumor has it that hard liquor will no longer be served to "our boys." Dummies, what do they think we are fighting for – if not for booze and broads?"'

Abel L. Dolim

'Instead of doing our homework we would sit at the runway threshold in the evenings and at weekends and watch the bombers land. We were called "little limeys". I got to know three crews very well. They were billeted in the field across from my parents' house. One hut had paintings of a B-17 and half-naked women on the walls behind their beds.'

Twelve-year-old Jim Matsell

Little Bo Peep has lost her sheep and doesn't know where to find her clothes!

'The 'Four Overs' arose from jealousy. People who were "hungry" saw the Americans as over fed. People who were "poorer" saw them as over paid. People who were "reserved" saw them as over sexed. None of this would have happened if they had not been over here, the British thought.' **Twelve-year old schoolgirl Helen Chipperfield**

'All the teenage girls were looking at the Americans in their uniforms and the Americans had more money than we did to spend on chocolates, flowers and stockings. They could even finagle a silk parachute, which could be used to make underwear.'

Twenty-year-old Philip Sage

Opposite: Mermaid and Sailor mural at Bungay (Flixton). The base was used by American Liberator bombers but in the winter of 1945-46 it became HMS *Europa* and then with the departure of the Fleet Air Arm, Flixton reverted to the RAF before finally closing in 1955.

Pin-up at Shipdham inspired by a Gillette A. 'Gil' Elvgren model, many of which appeared in various painted poses on popular pin-up calendars. Elvgren was famous in his own right for soft, warm Coca-Cola advertisements of the 1940s and after the war.

'When Sam and I first moved in, the pin-up girls were a pretty lecherous lot. About one in five owned a brassiere. Some of them blew down when the windows were open, some of them we took down when we showed the room to a couple of nurses, so that after a while we had a pretty nice bunch of girls, as nice as the ones in Fletch's room across the hall... Above my sack, climbing, there was a picture of Margaret Sullivan with bangs, a picture of Jane Russell with legs, a picture of a little dream dame called Doris Merrick...and she came out in *Yank*... She had a sort of what-the-hell look on her face and I used to dream about going back to Hollywood and meeting her in a drugstore on Sunset after she had finished at the studio...I said good-night to her the last thing every night.'

Bert Stiles

Nude that once adorned the briefing hut at Raydon in the Second World War and is now stored at Duxford.

'A fair imitation of a movie theater was maintained on the base and we saw many old pictures and some new ones. Monthly dances were held, where our own orchestra, the "Airliners" played and the base trucks brought the girls from Norwich and took them home – most of them. USO shows came occasionally, weekly "situation" talks were given, beer nights were held in the clubs and Special Services and the Red Cross kept us sane.'

Allan Healy

'One of our hutmates visited another base and on Sunday morning was in the latrine shaving when a couple of girls walked in and started brushing their teeth with soap. They quickly accepted his offer of a little toothpaste.'

Ronald D. Spencer

A pin-up now displayed at the 100th Bomb Group Memorial Museum at Thorpe Abbots.

'Hey Paw, tell me again how you and the boys were sweatin' it out in the ETO in England in 42, 43, 44, 45!' Mural in the 14th CBW area at Shipdham.

Eagle spreads its wings in the old Ground Officers' Mess at Wendling. Just after the war this building, which is now used by a Jaguar car spares business and which contains pin-ups and the B-24 silhouettes and eagle, was occupied by the Gilbert family who were evacuated to Wendling airfield after being bombed out in Norwich during the Baedeker Blitz. The mural was revealed when a false wall was removed where the American bar had been. In other rooms there are traces of the black mission board, pin-ups, the outline of a P-47 and other items.

The former movie theatre at Debach airfield near Clopton, Suffolk by Grove Farm, where 'Helton's Hellcats' of the 493rd Bomb Group were based during 1944-45.

'The theater was a large Nissen hut, perhaps 100 feet long. About 20 feet or so at the back was raised a couple of feet and was reserved for the officers. Hanging from the ceiling just in front of the officers' section was a small platform for the projector and the hapless projectionist. He had a ladder, which he used to climb up to the platform, which he then pulled up and stowed, on the platform during the showing of the film. This served two purposes. It prevented the audience from stealing the ladder, thereby marooning the projectionist on the platform. It also prevented the audience from reaching and inflicting bodily harm on the projectionist. The arrangement did not, however, stop the audience from throwing things at him and generally harassing him to the point of total exasperation. Fortunately (for us) film breakage and other malfunctions were the norm. When this occurred everyone began shouting obscenities at the projectionist. Fortunately for us he had absolutely no sense of humor and would start yelling back at the audience, advising that the film would not proceed until everyone quieted down. He would then fold his arms and stare straight ahead, making no effort to fix the problem. At this point the theater was total bedlam with the air filled with assorted garbage. Obviously, when a rare good picture was available the audience was a model of decorum. With the more common B pictures the place was a total zoo.

One memorable night an actor in the film accidentally killed a young lady, whereupon he more or less looked at the camera and spoke the world's greatest straight line, "what'll I do?" As might be expected, the audience had a number of rather carnal suggestions – one of the better being that he might consider doing something before she got cold.

It was all good fun and no one really cared one way or the other since the primary purpose was really to keep us out of bed or out of trouble.'

Ronald D. Spencer

FIVE – The Stately Dromes of England

The site of Oulton airfield, largely in the parish of Oulton Street, was requisitioned early in 1940 and opened in July as a satellite landing ground for Horsham St Faith. The majority of the aircrews initially were housed in local dwellings while a fortunate few were billeted in Blickling Hall nearby.

Nissen hut by the village pond at Oulton Street
to the east of the B1149 Norwich to Holt road.

'Oulton was the place we returned to when we'd been airborne for a while. To go to work every morning, we left our 'homes' at Blickling and rode by bus up to the Flights at Oulton. Blickling was our home in effect. Our Officers' Mess was only about 100-150 yards clear of the box hedges of Blickling Hall and our Nissen hut billets only another 200 yards further on. When we wanted to have a bath, we walked over to Blickling Hall and up to the top floor of the old mansion where we got a cold (make that, frigid) bath. Sometimes, during the morning or afternoon, if things were slack, we'd walk off the station, out past the guard-room and just across to the opposite side of the road to the Post Office there, where we would buy a cup of tea and a muffin or scone.'

Canadian Flight Lieutenant Murray Peden DFC QC, pilot, 214 Squadron

Deserted and overgrown, the runway at Oulton is home to poultry houses.

Sometimes known as Egmere, this Norfolk airfield 5 miles northwest of Fakenham and 2 miles east of North Creake village was on an area of farmland known as Bunker's Hill with the camp on the east side. The road from Burnham Thorpe to Little Walsingham running across the airfield site was closed. Although most of the runways have long since been removed, hangars and smaller buildings and parts of the perimeter track survive. The former technical site buildings are used by a feed mill operation. The watch office is now a private residence.

Great Massingham's sole remaining though weather-beaten T2 hangar and a cobweb-ridden and rusty piece of agricultural machinery, which continue to survive the ravages of harsh Norfolk winters, pictured in November 2005. This airfield, directly adjacent to the picturesque village with a large pond and delightful little shops was built in 1940 as a satellite for West Raynham 2 miles away. The Fox and Pheasant (the 'Poxy Pheasant') and Royal Oak, popular wartime pubs in Great Massingham, are now private residences. Now a private airfield, it is easily accessible as part of the perimeter track is a public footpath.

The watch office at Ludham, now a Grade II listed building, has been purchased by a KLM airline pilot whose intention is to turn it into a holiday home.

'American airmen were very generous. They gave the local children lovely Christmas parties and played Santa for them. They had things we didn't because everything was rationed. They gave us ice cream and peanut butter. I had never had peanut butter before. One night Glenn Miller's band played in the hangar at Great Ashfield airfield. I met an American flier and we danced to all the big hits. The next week I didn't see the young man about so I asked one his mates. "Oh he went off on a mission and didn't come back", he said. It was very sad.'

Margaret Robinson
Bury St Edmunds teenager

Jeepers creepers! Construction of Foulsham airfield 15 miles northwest of Norwich in the parishes of Wood Norton and Foulsham and a half mile north of the village of the same name began in 1941 and was almost complete by the late summer of 1942.

The Horsham St Faith Officers' Mess off Fifers Lane, Hellesdon (now Norwich Airport) shortly before it was demolished to make way for a housing development.

'The airfield at Horsham St Faith was really an attractive place, well kept and well landscaped. The permanent buildings were attractive. We had lucked out on a place to be stationed.'

Jackson Granholm

At various times during the Second World War Langham airfield was used by aircraft for anti-shipping strikes in the North Sea and off the enemy coast, and the rare dome, which was an astro trainer for night navigation was cosmetically restored in 1999.

'"Gentlemen, our target for tonight is Essen."

'Glug! Our hearts dropped. There it lay, at the end the red ribbon delineating our route, passing through the massed, red hatched areas indicating the heavy anti-aircraft defences and fighters of the Kammhuber Line, which protected the interior of Germany from Denmark to southeast of Paris. The section passing around the Ruhr, the most heavily defended of all.

We listened half-heartedly to the intelligence briefing on the defences, which, as always, was optimistic. We knew what they were really like and didn't need to be told by an ancient, non-flying officer what he imagined was in store for us.

The weather was good. Take off was to be at 1900.

Briefing over, we left for our messes once more to partake of our operational meal, always of real eggs and real bacon, unavailable to almost anyone else in wartime UK except through the black market. They were fattening us up for the kill.

Leaving the mess we returned to flights to prepare for take off time. This waiting time was always the worst period…'

Ron Read

Wartime hut and modern turkey sheds side by side at Attlebridge airfield, which was built in the parish of Weston Longville during 1941-42 and was used by RAF, Flying Dutchmen and American bomber crews. The airfield was sold in 1962 and Bernard Matthews Ltd began using the runways for turkey rearing operations and the buildings for administrative purposes.

P-51D Mustang *Big Beautiful Doll* passing Eye (Brome) airfield.

All along the watch tower at quaintly named Little Snoring airfield north of the A148 and east of the Little to Great Snoring road.

'I remember hearing the bombers leave and counting them coming in over the field early next day. Sometimes we lost a lot of friends and you could see WAAFs red-eyed from weeping for one special boy. A terrible loss of human life, but you had to carry on with what had to be done.'

Daphne Smith

Left and below:

History repeating itself. At Little Snoring longbowmen once practiced their archery skills in firing butts. Time marched on and by the mid 1940s this remote North Norfolk outpost was filled with a procession of Lancaster bombers departing on nocturnal sorties and Mosquito fighter bombers setting off on day and night intruder operations. The village sign at Snoring includes a propeller and Mosquito aircraft.

'The first Lancaster was given the "Green Light" from the mobile watchtower and we watched as it slowly climbed away. The remainder all slowly moved around the perimeter track towards the runway and then it was their turn for destination Berlin! The smoke from the engines and the smell of burning high-octane fuel eddied across the airfield.'

Sergeant Roland A. Hammersley DFM,
Lancaster WOP-AG

The Yellow Brick Road. Remains of an air raid shelter at Matlaske, a remote Norfolk airfield and a satellite for RAF Coltishall.

Fragment from a strip of American made Universal Pierced Steel Planking which was often laid on grass runways and taxiways to help prevent aircraft from becoming bogged down. Farmers are still unearthing pieces such as this one at Matlaske, during winter ploughing. Despite the PSP Matlaske airfield was often waterlogged and on occasion operations had to be switched to Swannington.

'Being on a squadron was to be quite remote from the rest of the world. It became your whole way of life, an enclave that occupied every member of it. Although we shared the airfield with a squadron of Lancasters, they might have been in the next county as far as we were concerned. We met them for a pint or two in the mess from time to time and swapped experiences but other than that their existence there might have been purely coincidental. I suppose they felt the same about us. There was a life going on outside the main gates of the airfield but we knew little of it. Our days revolved around the Battle Order, which was circulated each morning. Our days off were spent mainly in catching up with sleep or roistering in the mess or in our favourite pubs.'

Sergeant Johnnie Clark, Mosquito navigator

Martlesham Heath aerodrome was the proving ground of hundreds of different aircraft types and the station was also heavily involved in the development of radar. During the war years, Martlesham became an operational fighter station, first with the RAF and later with the USAAF. A number of industries now occupy the old hangars and buildings and a housing development has swallowed up much of the old aerodrome but there is still the occasional fly by.

Construction of Hethel airfield, 4 miles east of Wymondham and 7 miles from Norwich, began in August 1942 and was expanded early in 1943 to match the specifications needed to operate the heavy bombers of the 8th Air Force. Three hangars were built on the eastern side and the grounds of Stanfield Hall became the location for the bomb dump. Quarters were built to accommodate 395 officers and 2679 enlisted men. In November 1966 Lotus founder, Colin Chapman, moved his road and racecar factory from Cheshunt in Hertfordshire to the airfield where part of the runways are used as a test track. In Hethel Wood opposite is a completely restored gymnasium and chapel with surviving wall art and is now a museum commemorating the 389th Bomb Group.

Foulsham

Many Americans learned to ride bicycles and the locals thought it 'awfully funny' to see some of them learning. They mostly landed on their knees with the bike on top of them. When they could ride quite well they carried others on the crossbars and one often saw two or three on one bike. They found it difficult to remember to cycle on the left side of the road.

'…The base was so spread out it was difficult to get around without a jeep or a bike. The English summer was at its height, though it never really got warm enough according to my idea of summer. The air was fresh and cool, like a day of spring at home and the woods which were scattered all over our airdrome were beautiful. Through the woods small lanes were cut leading to the various living sites. I found in those first days in England many of the acquaintances of my early years: there were rooks and jackdaws flying overhead and grouse, plover and pheasants in great numbers just off the runways.

The second afternoon I was in England I rode my bike into the small village of Wymondham (pronounced Windum) near the field and was impressed by its picturesqueness. The lane leading into the village was narrow and winding, with hedgerows on either side and well-kept fields over the hedgerows. There were haystacks in the fields that were so perfectly formed they looked like loaves of gingerbread.'

Philip Ardery

110

To permit the building of runways at Swannington the village road to Brandiston had to be closed and the Cawston to Horsford road cut south of St Peter's Church, Haveringland, which today remains a solitary edifice on an otherwise featureless landscape. Flying Officer Jeffery N. Edwards, a navigator who with his pilot was killed one night in December 1944 when their Mosquito crashed while attempting to land, is buried in the churchyard. The airfield was sold in 1957 when it reverted to agricultural use with much of the concrete broken up for hardcore and a seed-packing firm acquired the technical site. The 'Hun score-board' showing some of 85 and 157 Mosquito Squadrons' victories, is now on display at the City of Norwich Museum.

Wratting Common airfield. This bomber airfield on the Cambridgeshire side of the boundary with Suffolk in the parishes of West Wickham and Little Thurlow, 3 miles northwest of Haverhill, was officially named West Wickham when it was built in 1942-43. After the war Wratting Common was soon reclaimed for agriculture with much of the concrete taken for hard core. The hangars survived, as did many of the larger Nissen huts. Most of the site is part of Thurlow Estates owned by the Vestey family.

Fersfield airfield, Norfolk, still remarkably recognisable one year into the new millennium.

Spindly limbs entwined around concrete huts on the old East Anglian airfields continue to spread in all directions like the tentacles of a devouring monster.

'…In the twilight of that evening almost at midnight, we heard a low throb begin in the sky above and grow to a mighty crescendo. In the bar, when the sound began, the song stopped a moment. We listened and someone said, "The RAF's out again. God bless 'em." I walked outside to see, but against the darkening sky the big black airplanes, Halifaxes and Lancasters, scarcely showed up at all. They were evidently going over at medium altitude, and they flew in a peculiar manner not at all like our formations. Still, it was a discernable pattern with distances of about half a mile between airplanes. Sometimes I could pick out a ship, but not many. I felt intense gratitude to those hardy lads going out just as we were having a final beer before going to bed. They were fighting a tough war and had been for a long time. Theirs was a beautiful country, and one could understand their determination to defend it.'

Philip Ardery

Villa-style watch tower at Swanton Morley airfield and now a Grade II listed building.

'Dining-in nights in Sergeants' and Officers' Messes have always been occasions for high jinks! When the formality of dinner was finished all manners of games were played. After a dinner in the Sergeants' Mess and following the usual capers, there was a 250cc DR motorcycle race around the anteroom! Another bit of nonsense was the challenge to hang upside-down by the crook of one's legs from a high open rafter of the mess anteroom and drink a pint of bitter.'

Group Captain Jack A. V. Short

Oulton basking in unseasonable Norfolk sunshine.

'The Officers' Mess was an imposing three-storeyed building built during the 1936 RAF expansion programme. Cars that were sprinkled around the car park were mainly pre-war vehicles such as "E"-type Morrises, early Fords, Hillmans and Standards. One chap had a nice little Austin 7, which was his pride and joy. A dozen of his fellow officers went outside and managed to lift the little car up the steps and into the entrance hall. When the officer blew his top, the culprits carried the little car back down the steps again!'

Group Captain Jack A. V. Short

Deopham Green airfield near Hingham, Norfolk has returned to agricultural use. There is a memorial to the 452nd Bomb Group whose Fortresses occupied the airfield in the Second World War and the original memorial plaque is at Attleborough railway station. In the early 1630s a number of inhabitants and their Parson, Robert Peck, sought religious freedom in America giving the name of their former home to Hingham, Massachusetts. Samuel Lincoln was baptized at Hingham church and later became apprenticed to a Norwich weaver. In the spring of 1638 he and his master sailed from Great Yarmouth to arrive in Salem at the end of June. He then moved to Hingham, Massachusetts where several generations later Abraham Lincoln was born.

Originally, the airfield at Wendling in the parish of Beeston near East Dereham was intended for RAF bomber use but in 1943 it was turned over to the 8th Air Force. The airfield was sold in 1963-64 and became a Bernard Matthews turkey farm with long turkey sheds being constructed on the runways.

'Having formed up the parade was brought to attention and "open order" by the adjutant and handed over to the new, nervous, station commander for inspection. His first task was to prepare the parade for an address by the padre. Unfortunately he issued the never-to-be-forgotten command: "Fall out Romans, Catholics, Jews and other denominations!"'

Group Captain Jack A. V. Short

'On my first visit to the cinema in Ipswich I was surprised to find people smoking inside. This was not allowed in the US. Another surprise I had was the reaction of the audience when an air raid warning was flashed on the screen. Nobody moved; they just carried on watching the film. Even when the "red-alert" was flashed on the screen nobody left. I sat tight, albeit somewhat nervous. Fortunately no bombs were dropped near the cinema. After going to see a film or just spending some time in Ipswich, hot fish and chips, wrapped in a newspaper English-style was good eating.'

Raymond G. Dozier, assistant engineering officer

Watching developments. Rougham airfield east of Bury St Edmunds under threat from the march of time. Bury St Edmunds was the capital of the Anglo-Saxon kingdom of East Anglia and later the seat of a very powerful monastery. In the Second World War it was a part of 'Little America', as the American bases were collectively known.

'…The food was horrible and we were warned time and time again, don't eat any kind of English sausage. The only bad part about going into an English pub, the beer was warm. Americans like cold beer… I really didn't get the chance too much to see London because we were too busy flying. Mainly when we were "home" we did a lot of sleeping. Going out was such a hassle anyway.'

Staff Sergeant Robert 'Bob' L. Schroeder, top turret gunner

Hardwick (Topcroft) airfield viewed though the nose of the BBMF Lancaster in September 1999.

Swanton Morley, once the largest RAF grass airfield in Europe.

'Operations, briefing rooms and squadron operations huts were all down on the flight line. This was about a half mile from the billeting area and we either cut through the woods or rode our bicycles to get there, except for combat missions when they sent trucks to the hut area for us…There were three runways, the longest was 6000 feet, and the other two shorter ones were 4800. We always used the longer runway for combat operations since we needed all of it taking off with full gas tanks and a load of bombs. The control tower was on the west side of the field just inside the perimeter track. The perimeter track was a continuous cement taxiway, 50 feet wide, that circled the entire airfield and it could be followed from any hardstand to the end of any runway. The hardstands, where the planes were parked were cement half circles that protruded like blisters along the perimeter track at odd intervals. This dispersed the aircraft in case of enemy attack and it allowed planes to leave their hardstands in the required order for mission takeoff and assembly.'　　　　　　　　　　　　　**Lieutenant (later Captain) Ralph Elliott**

Weeds growing in front of forlorn fuel tanks at Mendlesham airfield beside the A140 Norwich to Ipswich road and which nowadays is easy to spot for miles around because of the large television transmitter mast. By the roadside is an impressive memorial to the 34th Bomb Group built in 1949.

'Father says to the old boy, "Can you tell us the way to the aerodrome?"

The old man replies, "Aerodrome, what aerodrome?"

"Thorpe Abbotts old man."

"Thorpe Abbotts; where do you come from?"

"Metfield aerodrome."

"Yes but where do you come from?"

"Southwold," says father.

"How do I know that?" says the old man.

Father showed him his driving licence.

"How do I know that's not a forgery?" says the old man.

Father then said, "How do I know that you are not a spy?"

"Do I look like a spy?" asks the old man.

"Do I look like a spy?" asks father.

The old man replies, "Well no".

So father says, "Then tell us the way to the aerodrome," which the old man then proceeded to do.'

John Goldsmith and his father were trying to find their way to Thorpe Abbots airfield.

The fire pool, which was a feature of every base and quite often was used for the ceremonial dunking of lucky combat airmen on completion of their tours!

124

The watch tower at Langham airfield where turkey rearing sheds, part of the Bernard Mathews empire, have been built on the concrete areas except for the NE/SW runway. Other unused sections of concrete were broken up in 1985 for road construction.

'We arrived with three other crews. Later in the Mess Hall we learned that four crews failed to return on this day from Poznan, Poland. Such news to hear on arrival. For the month of April 25 crews were lost. What would our fate be?'

Wilbur Richardson, gunner, 94th BG

'The weather is going to be very hard to get used to. It's very damp and you seldom see the sun...'

**USAAF Sergeant in a letter to his wife
in California, October 1944**

Sculthorpe airfield, situated between the village of the same name and Syderstone to the west, north of the A148 Fakenham to King's Lynn road, was built during 1942-43 and was used by RAF, Free French and American units. Post war Sculthorpe became a USAF base. At Hunstanton, there is a memorial listing all those killed in the North Sea floods of 31 January 1953. It includes seventeen American airmen from Sculthorpe. At the end of 1992 the USAF withdrew and the base closed. The housing, mostly bungalows, built for USAF personnel and now known as Wicken Green Village, was sold in the mid-1990s.

Stearmans skirting Watton airfield. This 250-acre airfield was built in 1938-39 for the RAF who operated from the station until August 1942 when it was re-allocated to the USAAF. Now part of the Stanford Battle Training Area (STANTA), the main airfield site is off limits but many ex-wartime buildings such as the NAAFI and accommodation blocks on the opposite side of the Norwich-Watton road have been modified for industrial and commercial use.

Living sites contained separate quarters with detached WCs and ablutions. Though only expected to last for the duration of the war, buildings like these still survive, albeit with crumbling brick and ivy encrusted walls and they are slowly being eaten away like a cruel sea eroding a once proud coastline.

'In the Enlisted Men's Bar and Lounge the hardy still drank their beer night after night in a room made pleasanter by the addition of two large home-made stoves, watching the gamblers at the dice table and the optimists at the slot machines. Eyebrows were raised when on successive nights the same man hit two jackpots. Eyebrows were raised even higher when it was discovered that the winner was Cpl Walter C. Ruhland: organist and clerk in the Chaplain's office.'

John S. Sloan

Shipdham and the old technical site with the control tower in the snow.

'On Christmas Eve, when aircraft of the Group had been diverted to other fields because of weather conditions, two swans elected to be diverted to the base. MPs on duty at the main gate were startled by an unfamiliar and sustained noise, followed by a slight jolt against the side of the MP hut. Investigation produced a slightly dazed, icy-winged swan, which, apparently attracted by light, had flown against the side of the hut. Minutes later another swan came down, this time a few yards away. Mystified but not intimidated by this unusual circumstance the MPs solved the dilemma in a traditional MP way and the visitors were escorted to the guardhouse. In the morning they were released.'

John S. Sloan

Lavenham in Suffolk is perhaps the best preserved medieval town in Britain, a centre of the medieval wool and cloth industry where the lath-and-plaster timber-framed dwellings, so typical of this area, are numerous. Among the finest is the Guildhall in the main square (top left). Along with Long Melford, 3 miles to the west, Lavenham has a parish church of outstanding beauty and craftsmanship. The adjacent airfield is well commemorated by plaques in the square, church and the Swan Inn.

"Some day you should go over the hills to Lavenham – there's the most beautiful little Elizabethan village in England. The old Guildhall, the beautiful lath-and-plaster houses, all bright pink and yellow, the wool church. And there's one man left of the old wool-weavers, one man who carried on the trade that made Lavenham rich and famous! You can still buy from him (if you could get the coupons and if he has the material) the real English home spun tweeds – and there's none finer in the world! Some Sunday we'll go out to Lavenham on our bicycles and I'll show you around the town and we'll have a drink at "The Swan" – there's a real old English inn for you!'

Vivian Goodman talking to American Robert S. Arbib Jr, author of
Here We Are Together: The Notebook of an American Soldier in Britain.

RAF and American airmen's signatures in the Swan Inn (now a hotel) at Lavenham.

Reflections in time. Lavenham control tower.

'The country of East Anglia is well endowed with historic old inns and most of them have preserved the Olde Englishe Quaintnesse one expects to find nowadays on Christmas cards and in antique prints... In the little region of Suffolk that I knew best, the tourist guides undoubtedly point out as rare treasures "The Bull" at Long Melford, the Lavenham "Swan", the Thetford "Bell"(across the line in Norfolk) and the Martlesham "Red Lion", the Woodbridge "Crown" and the Bury St Edmund's "Angel". In all of these and many more, you can find the low-beamed ceilings, the capacious fireplaces, the polished copper saucepans on the wall, the hunting prints, the winding, uneven staircases and the leaded diamond windows that are so dear to British hearts and the LNER poster artists.'

Robert S. Arbib Jr.

131

Shepherds Grove airfield northeast of Ixworth in Suffolk was built for American use in 1943 but opened as a RAF airfield in 1944 as a satellite for Stradishall. After being used as a Thor missile base the airfield reverted to civilian use in 1963.

'I was now an old combat veteran and though only twenty-one-years old, I had seen enough for a lifetime. I had literally grown up in the war. More of my friends were dead than alive. A seemingly endless procession of crews had come and gone out of our squadron. Only a handful of them had completed a tour of operations.' **Ben Smith Jr., radio operator**

Tempsford airfield, which snuggles in a shallow valley straddling the Hertfordshire/Bedfordshire county border 4½ miles south of St Neots and a mile from the Al trunk road and Tempsford village, covered 500 acres, largely in the parish of Everton. Gibraltar Farm, on the eastern side of the airfield (centre, right) came to be isolated within the perimeter track and the barn was used as the holding point for SOE (Special Operations Executive) operatives before they boarded aircraft to parachute them into occupied countries. Here the agents – male and female – made their last checks before leaving, many of them never to return. This building has been preserved and a plaque inside recalls their brave deeds.

Bury St Edmunds (Rougham) airfield. The control tower museum is now a Grade II listed building. Many famous people visited Rougham during the war years including General Montgomery and Charles de Gaulle and entertainers such as Bob Hope, Frances Langford, Clark Gable and the Glenn Miller band, playing for the 200th mission party in one of the hangars. On part of the former airfield is the Flying Fortress pub.

Lavenham airfield near the famous old wool town 11 miles south of Bury St Edmunds.

'We stood at the front gate in a row while Bob walked past, shaking hands with each of us in turn. "Good-byes," "Good Lucks" and "Thank Yous" were said. Bob walked off along the road and I had to turn away to hide the tears which blinded me as I walked back to the house. The end – for a time – of a perfect friendship.'

Fourteen-year-old schoolgirl Primrose Henderson-Gray

BBMF Spitfire XIX photographed from the rear turret of Lancaster BI on Battle of Britain Day, 15 September 1999 with Eye airfield, one mile southwest of Brome in Suffolk on the Norwich to Ipswich road. Eye was an American bomber base in the Second World War and post war it reverted to agriculture. In recent years a waste reclamation site (bottom right quadrant) has been built on the site.

Earls Colne airfield south of the Essex village was used by the Americans from 1943 until the summer of 1944 when it reverted to RAF use for SOE and, later, glider operations. The RAF left in 1946 and the base reverted to agricultural land until it was redeveloped as a site for a golf and leisure complex.

Shades of Jimmy Stewart. Taking off from the former wartime American base at Old Buckenham. A party for 1250 local children and London Blitz orphans was held at Old Buckenham on Christmas Eve 1944.

'Clear warm sunshine flooded the silent field. Here, where thousands of take-offs and landings had been made, we found our reason for coming. Silent tribute was paid to hundreds of our companions who never returned. We were remembering the heavily loaded ships that crashed at the end of the runway on take-off, the exploding bombs, the clouds of black smoke; the crippled B-24s that had found their way home only to crash-land and burn. We remembered seeing our friends shot out of the sky over Germany – of the empty beds in those cold Nissen huts after a rough mission. Yes, we trembled inside. Grown men with hot tears burning our eyes. All those memories were fresh now.'
Milton R. Stokes, pilot

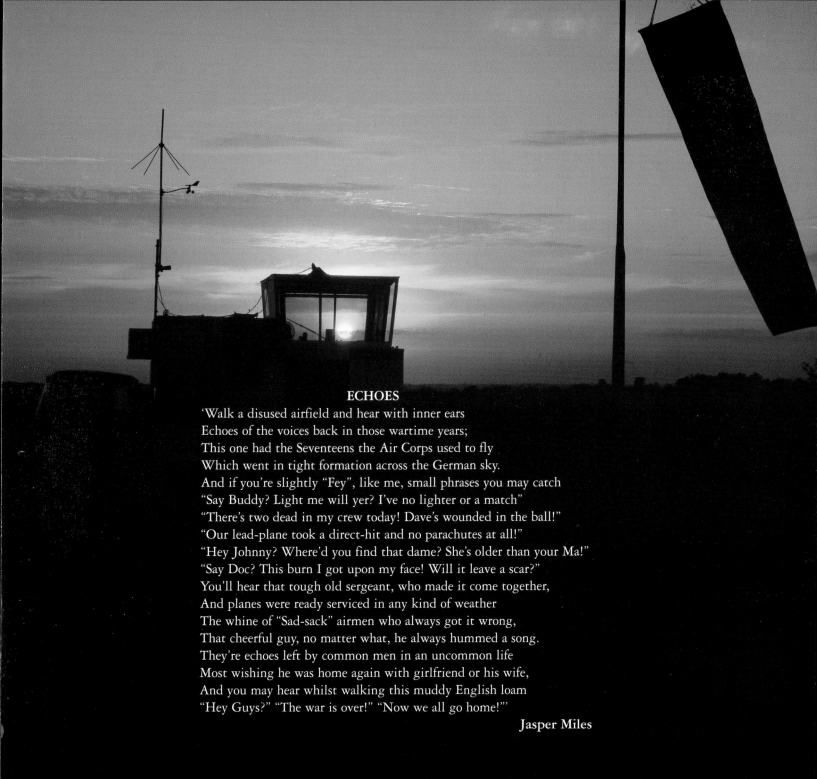

ECHOES

'Walk a disused airfield and hear with inner ears
Echoes of the voices back in those wartime years;
This one had the Seventeens the Air Corps used to fly
Which went in tight formation across the German sky.
And if you're slightly "Fey", like me, small phrases you may catch
"Say Buddy? Light me will yer? I've no lighter or a match"
"There's two dead in my crew today! Dave's wounded in the ball!"
"Our lead-plane took a direct-hit and no parachutes at all!"
"Hey Johnny? Where'd you find that dame? She's older than your Ma!"
"Say Doc? This burn I got upon my face! Will it leave a scar?"
You'll hear that tough old sergeant, who made it come together,
And planes were ready serviced in any kind of weather
The whine of "Sad-sack" airmen who always got it wrong,
That cheerful guy, no matter what, he always hummed a song.
They're echoes left by common men in an uncommon life
Most wishing he was home again with girlfriend or his wife,
And you may hear whilst walking this muddy English loam
"Hey Guys?" "The war is over!" "Now we all go home!"'

Jasper Miles

Knettishall memorial dedication.

ACKNOWLEDGEMENTS

Jim Avis; Dave Bagshaw; Ed Boulter DFC; John Carter; Tom Chilton; Forrest S. Clark; George M. Collar; Abel L. Dolim; Bill Espie; Dale Featherby; Gene Gaskins; Jim Gintner; Larry Goldstein, President, 8th AFHS; Primrose Henderson-Gray; John A. Holden; Gerry Honey OBE; Keith Lawrence; Brian H. Mahoney; Steve Mendham; Bruce Monk; Jim 'Dinty' Moore DFC; Jack Peppiatt; Ron Read; Wilbur Richardson; Penny Riches; Bill Rose; Frank Sherman; Group Captain J. A. V. Short; Alvin Skaggs; Ben Smith Jr.; William C. Stewart; Milton R. Stokes; Group Captain A. F. Wallace; Joe Wroblewski.

A snowbound Swanton Morley in the
last months of RAF occupancy.

BIBLIOGRAPHY

Airfields of 100 Group, Martin W. Bowman. Pen & Sword 2006.

Airfields of The 2nd Air Division, Martin W. Bowman. Pen & Sword 2006.

Airfields of The 1st Air Division, Martin W. Bowman. Pen & Sword 2007.

RAF Airfields of Norfolk, Martin W. Bowman. Pen & Sword 2007.

A Thousand Shall Fall, Murray Peden DFC QC. Canada's Wings 1979.

Country Boy, Combat Bomber Pilot, R. H. Tays. Privately Published 1990.

There we were…or The saga of crew No. 8. Ronald D. Spencer. Manuscript.

452nd BG History.

8th Air Force At War. Memories and Missions, England 1942-45. Martin W. Bowman. PSL 1994.

Battle-Axe Blenheims: No 105 Squadron RAF At War 1940-1, Stuart R. Scott Sutton 1996.

Bomber Pilot, Philip Ardery. The University Press of Kentucky, Lexington, Kentucky, 1978.

Bomber's Bombers Their Story in Verse, Jasper Miles.

Chick's Crew: A Tale of the Eighth Air Force, Ben Smith Jr. Privately Published 1978.

Churchill's Light Cavalry (2 Vols.), Jim Moore DFC.

Crew Sixty-Four, Gene Gaskins. Privately Published.

Echoes: A Tribute in Verse to the USAAC 1942-45, Jasper Miles.

Fields of Little America, Martin W. Bowman. Wensum Books 1977, PSL & GMS 2003.

First of the Many', Captain John R. 'Tex' McCrary and David E. Sherman. 1944.

First Over Germany: A History of the 306th Bomb Group, Russell A. Strong. 1982.

If You Can't Take a Joke, Ron Read DFC. Privately Published.

In Search of Peace, 453rd BG History. Mike Benarchik.

Into Battle With 57 Squadron, Roland A. Hammersley DFM. Privately published 1992.

Letters Home and Other Stuff, Major Ralph H. Elliott. Unpublished.

Light Perpetual: Aviators' Memorial Windows, David Beaty. Airlife 1995.

Low Level From Swanton, Martin W. Bowman. Air Research Publications 1995.

Mosquito Thunder, Stuart R. Scott. Sutton 1999.

One Man's War, Johnnie Clark. Privately Published by Ann Solberg Clark.

Reluctant Witness, James J. Mahoney and Brian H. Mahoney. Trafford Publishing 2001.

Serenade To The Big Bird, Bert Stiles.

Skyways to Berlin, Major John M. Redding & Captain Harold Leyshon. Bobbs Merrill 1943.

The 467th Bombardment Group. Allan Healy. Privately Printed 1947.

The Day We Bombed Switzerland – Flying with the US 8th AF in WWII, Jackson Granholm. Airlife 2000.

The Lucky Bastards, Abel L. Dolim. Manuscript.

The Men Who Flew the Mosquito, Martin W. Bowman. PSL 1995 Pen & Sword 2003.

The Route As Briefed. The history of the 92nd Bombardment Group USAAF 1942-45. John S. Sloan.

The Royal Air Force At War: Memories and personal experiences, 1939-present. PSL 1997.

The War At My Door,. Dick Wickham.

The Yanks Are Coming, Edwin R. W. Hale and John Frayn Turner. Midas Books 1983.

Twelve O'Clock High, Beirne Lay Jr and Sy Bartlett. Ballantine Books 1948.

Women In Air Force Blue, Squadron Leader Beryl E. Escott. PSL 1989.

Yesterday's Dragons: The B-17 Flying Fortress over Europe during WWII, Abel L. Dolim. 2001.

Flooded runway at Horham after the winter rains.

Spitfire and Lancaster of the BBMF passing Attlebridge
(Weston Longville) airfield on a summer's evening